OverTime

THE JAZZ *photographs of* MILT HINTON

Milt Hinton, David G. Berger
and Holly Maxson

POMEGRANATE ARTBOOKS SAN FRANCISCO

For Mona,
the developer
and the fixer

OverTime
The Jazz Photographs of
Milt Hinton

by Milt Hinton, David G. Berger
and Holly Maxson

Published by Pomegranate
Artbooks, Box 808022,
Petaluma, California 94975

Printed in Korea

FIRST EDITION

Contents

About My Life

by MILT HINTON

I was born at home in Vicksburg, Mississippi, on June 23, 1910. Our family lived in the black section of town, at the bottom of a hill, close to the banks of the Mississippi River. We rented a house that had two rooms. It was built on

Hilda Gertrude Robinson and son Milton, Vicksburg, Mississippi, c. 1911

stilts so when the river flooded the water could run underneath and we'd stay dry.

My parents split up before I was born, and there were no other children. I lived with my mother, two of her sisters and my grandmother. I was in my thirties when I met my father for the first time.

In 1919, when I was nine, our family moved north to Chicago. Two of my mother's brothers, my uncles Bob and Matt, had been living there for a few years. Like many other blacks back in those days, they had found good jobs in Chicago, and they were able to rent a beautiful apartment for us on the Southside of the city.

The Southside was an exciting place to grow up. Like my uncles, many blacks were able to get good jobs in the stockyards or in the fancy hotels and restaurants downtown. They were well off, especially compared with the way they had lived down South. Chicago became one of the country's leading centers for black culture and entertainment.

There were great theaters in my neighborhood—the Vendome, the Metropolitan and the Michigan—where performers like Louis Armstrong, Duke Ellington, Fess Williams, Erskine Tate and Sammy Stewart played. And there were famous nightclubs—the Sunset Cafe, the Entertainers and the Golden Lily—which featured the best bands, such as Fletcher Henderson, Andy Kirk, Earl Hines and McKinney's Cotton Pickers. I'd spend most Sunday afternoons at one of the theaters, and sometimes on my way home from school I'd peep through a door and watch the musicians rehearsing at one of the clubs.

My mother played piano for our church's choir, but she always wanted me to study violin. I think she got the idea from seeing violin players in all the theater orchestras on the Southside. They were distinguished-looking black gentlemen who had made it to the top.

I got my first violin in 1923 on my thirteenth birthday. I began taking lessons in the back room of

Hilda Gertrude Robinson, Ed Burke and Milt Hinton, Chicago, c. 1923

a local music store, but soon my mother found me a great teacher, Professor James Johnson. He was a well-educated man who really taught me the fundamentals of my instrument. I was also fortunate to attend Wendell Phillips High School, which had a strong music program and some very talented students.

I played violin in the school orchestra, but sometime around my sophomore year I decided to join the marching band. They had military uniforms and played at all the football games, and the girls always seemed to be more interested in the guys in the band. Back in those days, a

Wendell Phillips H.S. Marching Band (Milt Hinton, top row left, with tuba), Chicago, c. 1929

boy with a name like Milton who was really skinny and carried a violin around all day had to try just about anything to be popular. Of course, the band didn't have violins, so I tried three or four brass instruments before one of the tuba players graduated and I took his place in the band.

The person who had the greatest influence on me musically during my high school days was Major N. Clark Smith, the band director. He always wanted perfection and he was a disciplinarian, but everyone respected him because he was such a great musician. He could play every instrument, make wonderful arrangements and write original music. I didn't know it back then, but I found out later that many well-known musicians had been influenced by him.

I've only had two jobs in my life—delivering newspapers in the neighborhood and playing music. I started getting work as a professional musician in my last year of high school. Dance bands around Chicago were hiring bass players because they wanted a softer sound, and because of my experience with the violin the transition to bass felt natural. I kept my paper route until my mother told me I could only work one job. At that point I was doing well enough in music, so the choice was clear.

After I finished high school, I studied music at Crane Junior College and then spent a short time at

Northwestern University. During those years I had a chance to play with jazz pioneers who lived and worked in Chicago: Freddie Keppard, Johnny Long, Tiny Parham, Cassino Simpson, Jabbo Smith and Erskine Tate. But the two musicians who influenced me most were Eddie South, the great violinist, and Louis Armstrong's famous drummer Zutty Singleton.

As a young boy studying violin, Eddie was my idol. Performing with him was a dream come true, and it gave me the chance to experience his musical genius firsthand. Zutty hired me for his band, which played at one of the best jazz clubs in Chicago — The Three Deuces. That's where Cab Calloway saw me for the first time one night in 1936 and gave me a job.

Cab was a singer and dancer who could entertain an audience better than anyone I ever saw. I stayed with the band until it broke up about fifteen years later. Throughout those years some of the greatest jazz musicians in the world played in the band, including Ben Webster, Chu Berry, Dizzy Gillespie, Cozy Cole and Illinois Jacquet.

We'd usually play the Cotton Club in New York City for five or six months. There would be a show that featured Cab along with our seventeen-piece band, singers, dancers and one or two comedians. Then we'd cross the country, spending a week or two playing big cities and one or two nights in smaller towns. We did radio broadcasts a couple of times a week from wherever we were playing. That gave us an even bigger following.

Milt Hinton, Hoover Dam, Arizona/Nevada, c. 1940

For years Cab was really one of the top acts in show business.

Wherever we went, we'd go in style. Cab bought us beautiful uniforms, and we always had a couple of valets with us who took care of everything from moving instruments to cleaning our laundry. Back in those days, in many towns both in the North and in the South, blacks weren't allowed to stay in nice hotels. But Cab was often able to get around the problem. Whenever we could travel by train, he'd rent a fancy railroad car that had sleeping berths for everyone in the band. Then when we'd stop to play in a city, he'd have our railroad car put on a side rail so we could use it instead of going to a second-rate hotel.

Of course, there were some problems concerning race that no one could get around, especially in the South. It didn't matter how famous you were or how much money you had. If you were black, you still had to eat in "colored" restaurants and use the "colored" entrance to railroad stations. When we played theaters in the South, whites would have one section of the seats and blacks would be in another area that was usually farther away from the stage.

A few times we played at dances where they'd actually stretch a rope down the middle of the floor to separate blacks and whites. Living in the North, the guys in the band would joke about the stupidity of these kinds of things. But inside I think each one of us really suffered because of them.

Cab made records with the band, but he always seemed to prefer radio. Fortunately for me, whenever I was in New York during the late '30s and early '40s I'd get calls to record with some of the musicians I'd known in Chicago. Many of the records I made with people like Billie Holiday, Ethel Waters, Coleman Hawkins, Benny Goodman, Benny Carter, Teddy Wilson, Lionel Hampton and Ben Webster have become classics. That's something that makes me very proud.

Playing the same tunes night after night in Cab's band wasn't very demanding. Many guys got so used to it that they stopped developing as musicians. But a few of us realized that being in the band gave us an opportunity to learn from each other. We'd create challenges for ourselves by changing arrangements and adding new ones. We'd be sure to practice almost every day, individually and with each other. And we also thought it was important to improve our ability to read music. I didn't know it then, but this kind of training is what really prepared me to work in the studios later in my career.

I met the real love of my life, Mona Clayton, in 1939 when she was singing in my mother's church choir. A short time later we were married. Mona had a profound influence on my life right from the start. We were inseparable. She trav-eled with the band wherever we went, and once she learned how things worked she was able to make a valuable contribution. This was particularly true when we played smaller towns where there weren't many hotels and restaurants serving blacks. Mona would find local people who would rent us rooms and fix meals for all the guys. Pretty soon everyone in the

Mona Clayton Hinton, Chicago, c. 1941

band came to appreciate her.

In 1947 our daughter, Charlotte, was born. At first she traveled with us, but it wasn't long before we realized that we couldn't take care of a

Milt Hinton and daughter Charlotte, Queens, New York, c. 1948

baby on the road. Within a year Mona managed to find a nice two-family house in Queens, New York, and we scraped together enough money to buy it. After all those years together, we couldn't adjust to being apart. But as it turned out we didn't have to for very long. Cab's work slowed down so much that by 1951 he was forced to break up the band.

For a few months I struggled finding work. With a wife and child to support and a house to pay for, I played anywhere I could. There were many nights when Danny Barker, my friend from Cab's band, and I would take the ferry to New Jersey and go from bar to bar playing for tips. Luckily, it wasn't long before another old friend from Cab's band, Cozy Cole, recommended me to Louis Armstrong.

Louis hired me and we spent a couple of months touring the country and playing all over Japan. Louis was from New Orleans, but he'd made his reputation in Chicago. He was a star I'd seen perform many times when I was still in knee pants. Playing on the same stage with him and getting to know him personally fulfilled a life-long ambition. And working alongside Barney Bigard—another big name I'd idolized as a kid—was an added bonus.

I left Louis when I was hired to be in the band on a CBS radio show broadcast from New York. I took the job because I wanted to be with my wife and daughter and because it was a day show, which gave me an opportunity to play other jobs at night. As it turned out, it was one of the wisest decisions I ever made. Within a few months I was working on a couple of other radio and TV shows, playing in different jazz clubs around the city, and beginning to get calls to play on record sessions.

Jackie Gleason is one of the people responsible for getting me into the recording studios. I knew him when he was just starting out as a comedian and struggling to get by. And he didn't forget his old friends. Years later, in the mid '50s, when he was successful, I ran into him on the street and he hired me to make a record with him. He must've had fifty string players at that session—violins, violas, cellos—and I got to meet some of the select group of musicians who made a living in the New York recording studios.

Once the people who did the hiring realized I was dependable and experienced and could read music, I began to get calls. Most of the musicians doing this kind of work were white, but my being on the scene didn't bother anyone. I was welcome just as long as I could do the job.

I spent about fifteen years freelancing in the studios. I made rock 'n' roll records with groups like the Drifters, the Coasters and the Isley Brothers; I accompanied popular stars like Harry Belafonte, Tony Bennett, Sam Cooke,

Milt Hinton, recording studio, New York, c. 1953

Sammy Davis, Jr., Patti LaBelle, Paul McCartney, Frank Sinatra and Barbra Streisand; and I made jazz records with Quincy Jones, Sarah Vaughan and Joe Williams, among others. I also got called to record music for commercials on radio and TV.

By the middle of the '60s the record business had slowed down. Our daughter was in college, and Mona and I managed to travel to some interesting places. I toured with Paul Anka, made trips to Russia and the Middle East with Pearl Bailey, and worked with Bing Crosby here and in England.

Around the same time I started getting more recognition in jazz circles. There were lots of calls to play at jazz festivals and parties around the country and overseas, and I was hired for more jazz records. I also started workshops for students at Hunter and Baruch Colleges in New York City and traveled to other schools to do clinics.

Today, Mona and I are still happily married.

Charlotte is settled in Atlanta with her husband, Bill Morgan, and their daughter, Inez Mona. I'm still very active—teaching, performing, making record dates and even doing a few movie soundtracks. As long as I'm standing, I'll be working. I don't ever want to retire.

A bright new group of jazz musicians is emerging. These are the people who challenge me most. I feel it's my duty to pass on to their generation what I've experienced and what I've learned. But they're really my teachers. They help me understand the present, and they're the ones who give me hope for the future.

On Photography

by MILT HINTON

*Milt Hinton, Hartford,
Connecticut, 1989
(photo by Bob Appleton)*

Bass Line, the book I wrote with my friend David Berger several years ago, is really the story of my life. And although it includes almost two hundred of the pictures I've taken, I didn't really deal with the subject of photography in that book. *OverTime* features my photographs—a completely different group of them—so it gives me a chance to talk about how I got involved in photography and how my interests developed through the years.

I got my first camera in 1935. It was a 35 mm Argus C-3, and it was a present for my twenty-fifth birthday. Just as soon as I had it unwrapped and put film in it, I started taking pictures of everyone and everything.

I had the Argus with me when I started on the road with Cab Calloway in 1936. Although I took a few posed shots, I was never much for taking formal pictures. Everybody was shooting the band on stage in uniform, and if you went to a professional photographer for your own publicity shot, he'd ask you to smile and put your horn up in the air. I've never wanted to get those kinds of photos because I've never seen musicians that way.

I always tried to capture something different. I'd sneak up on people and shoot them when they were off guard. Of course, I was limited to some extent. I didn't have a flash, and in those days the film speed was so slow that you couldn't take photographs indoors without using a long exposure. Even so, I did get some unusual indoor shots, like pictures of the guys in the band sleeping on the train.

Whenever I've wanted a photograph of a particular person, I've tried to shoot it in some kind of background context that has a special meaning for me. For example, years ago when I was in Springfield, Illinois, with Cab, I wanted a shot of the Lincoln statue. But instead of taking a picture of the statue itself, I got five or six shots from different angles, with Danny Barker standing out in front of it. I tried to do the same thing later on when I traveled to other countries.

Truthfully, I've always been biased toward black-and-white photography. I think it's because when I look at a color photo, I really don't see the same colors I see in nature. Besides, when I got started, color film faded badly after a short time.

Over the years I've been asked why I took some of the pictures I did. It's hard for me to answer that question. When I took early pictures of Dizzy Gillespie, we were both in Cab's band. Even back in those days I knew he was very innovative, but I never suspected he would turn out to be a jazz legend. The same is true for Chu Berry and Cozy Cole. These guys were my friends, and I wanted pictures of them so one day we could all look back and remember the times we'd shared when we were young.

When I shot Jim Crow signs in the South, I intended to be funny. I wasn't trying to prove anything. We all lived in the North, and one of the only ways we could deal with the stupidity of the segregation laws was to make fun of them.

At some point, probably in the late '40s, I began to realize that I was experiencing jazz history firsthand. The music was changing rapidly, and there were new faces coming on the scene constantly. Some of the pioneers, like Chu and Jimmy Blanton, were already gone, and some of the other greats were well on their way to early deaths. For some reason, I felt strongly about using my camera to capture the people and events from the jazz world that I was lucky enough to witness.

Keg Johnson, the great trombone player with Cab who was responsible for getting me into the band, had more influence on my photography than anyone else. He was diligent and precise with just about everything in his life, and even though he didn't have many personal possessions, whenever he did buy something it had to be the best. Consequently, a couple of years before the War, when he decided to get a camera, he bought the best Leica he could find. After that he spent weeks reading photography books and magazines.

I couldn't believe the kind of pictures he got with his Leica. Everything was absolutely needle sharp. I saw all kinds of new possibilities, and it wasn't long before I bought a Leica, too.

We decided to process our own film while we were traveling with Cab. We picked up a few instruction books and bought some basic equipment. We'd usually start late at night, after we finished playing the last show. That way we didn't have to figure out how to block off the light in our hotel room. I remember that before starting we'd each make a stack of the film we wanted to develop and the negatives we wanted to print. We'd bought a special box that allowed us to make a 4-x-5 print from a 35 mm negative. We'd work until daybreak when the room started getting light, and by the time we cleaned up it would be about seven in the morning. We'd get some breakfast, then go to sleep.

Keg and I never seemed to have enough time for our photography. It got to the point where I was shooting more film than I could get processed commercially. It started when we were doing one-nighters. I realized that in most cases a local drug-store couldn't get my film back to me before I'd have to leave the town. So when I'd finish shooting a roll of film, I'd throw it into a shoe box in my travel trunk. I figured I'd wait until I got back to New York and then have every-thing processed, but that rarely happened. Instead, I'd end up putting all my exposed rolls in a carton or a drawer. Most of them sat there for fifteen or twenty years.

In the early '50s, a short time after Mona and I bought our first house in Queens, I set up a dark-room in the basement. By this time I wasn't out on the road anymore, and I thought I'd be able to spend more time working on photographs. I got my first enlarger through a friend from Cab's band, Gene Mikell, who'd left

music and was working at the U.N. He told me they were replacing darkroom equipment and he could get me an Omega for a hundred dollars. I grabbed it.

When I went to Japan with Louis Armstrong in the early '50s, I bought a Canon 35 mm range-finder camera. It had advantages over the Leica; it was easier to load film, it had a mechanical trigger for advancing film, and when you changed lenses you could reset the eyepiece to get a better idea of what was included in the frame. Even though the Canon was easier to use, there was something unique about the pictures I got with the Leica, so I used both cam-eras. I'd usually keep one loaded with black-and-white and the other with color film. This went on until the early '60s, when I bought a single-lens reflex, a Nikon F. At that point, I put away both the Leica and the Canon.

When it comes to pho-tography, I don't think of

myself as an artist. I have no formal training, and I never had time to study on my own. Consequently, I don't have a foundation in the history of photography or a real knowledge of the giants in the field. Unfortu-nately, I wasn't able to devote enough time to developing my technique, either. But when I look at other people's pictures, I know what I like. And I do take pride in many of my photographs .

When I saw Billie Holi-day at what turned out to be her last recording ses-sions, I had a feeling she was close to the end. I think the record company people knew exactly what was going on and were try-ing to finish the album while she was still on her feet. Ray Ellis was the con-ductor, and evidently Billie had insisted on having the guys who'd worked with her over the years on the date. Al Cohn, Urbie Green, Hank Jones and Osie John-son were there, and I remember we had to reschedule a session because

Sweets Edison couldn't make it in from the West Coast on time.

The shots I got on one of those last dates were taken while Billie was lis-tening to playbacks. Look-ing at her, I could see how disappointed she was about how she sounded. I don't think it was her intonation or phrasing that bothered her. The quality of her voice was gone, and she knew it better than anyone. As she listened, her eyes would fill with tears, and I had the feeling she was imagining how she had sounded twenty years earli-er when she'd sung the same song. She seemed to be so wrapped up in listen-ing that she was completely unaware of me and my camera.

I'm also very pleased about some of the shots I got at the "Sound of Jazz" and Timex television shows. I think these were two of the best visual pre-sentations ever done on jazz. I was able to photo-graph Billie with Jo Jones, and I got shots of Louis

Armstrong and Bobby Hackett, Jackie Gleason, Dizzy and many of the giants in Duke Ellington's band.

In 1959, *Esquire* maga-zine invited practically every living jazz musician to pose for pictures up in Harlem. It was scheduled for 10:00 A.M. Even though the hour was early—espe-cially for jazz musicians—and there was no money involved, the turnout was enormous. The minute I arrived I knew it would be a big social event. Some of these people might work together from time to time or they'd run into each other in a bar, but to get sixty or seventy of them in one place at one time was truly amazing.

I don't think the *Esquire* people had any idea about the importance of the gathering. All they seemed to want was a perfect shot of the whole group, posed around the stoop of a brownstone building in Harlem. It was funny to watch the musicians frater-nizing while the magazine

people shouted directions at them.

Except for *Esquire* pho-tographer Art Kane, I don't remember any other people with cameras. For-tunately, I'd had enough sense to bring three—my Leica and Canon and a lit-tle Keystone 8 mm movie camera. I remember I gave Scoville Browne the Canon, which had color slide film in it, and Mona took color movies. I used the Leica, which was load-ed with black-and-white film.

It was one of those times when I felt the need to record an important event in the jazz world. I wanted future generations to be able to see some of the best representatives of the different eras of jazz all mingling together.

By the time I was play-ing in the studios regularly, I had one or two cameras with me all the time. Record companies had some great professional photographers come in and shoot sessions, but they kept a close watch on

Milt and Mona Hinton, Hartford, Connecticut, 1989
(Photo by Bob Appleton)

the things they'd allow them to do. They'd usually let them in at the beginning and end of a date, or on a couple of five-minute breaks. Sometimes they'd send in a makeup artist to work on the performer, and often they'd spend an hour setting up a shot to make it look candid.

Of course, as a musi-cian hired to play the date, I could get pictures when-ever I wanted. In fact, I don't think anyone ever stopped me during all those years. Chuck Stewart, a great photographer who worked for many of the jazz labels back in those days, used to kid me about my picture taking. He had seen me in the studios with my camera equipment, and he'd say, "One of these days I'm gonna get me a good bass, then we'll see how much work you get."

Whenever I had enough time, I'd develop my film and then make contact prints. I'd usually enlarge a few shots of some of the studio guys and give them copies the next time we worked together. After a while these shots got to be well known around the stu-dios, but there were always jokes about my printing. It seemed that whenever I made pictures of my white friends, I'd print them looking very dark. Guys would ask me about it, and I'd always give them the same answer: "I can't help it, that's just the way I see everybody."

The Milton J. Hinton Photographic Collection

by DAVID G. BERGER and HOLLY MAXSON

The black-and-white photographs taken by Milt Hinton between 1935 and the present are housed in The Milton J. Hinton Photographic Collection in Philadelphia. Maintained by David G. Berger and Holly Maxson, the collection contains approximately 40,000 35 mm negatives, 1,200 contact prints, 1,525 8-x-10-inch work prints and 120 11-x-14-inch exhibition-quality prints. Robert Asman, a gifted photographer based in Philadelphia, has been responsible for developing and printing Milt's work for nearly ten years.

Photographs from the collection are selectively made available to a wide variety of print publications including magazines, texts and record albums and to film and video producers as well. More than 175 photographs appeared in *Bass Line: The Stories and Photographs of Milt Hinton*, published by Temple University Press in 1988. And since 1989 Pomegranate Calendars & Books has published a yearly calendar featuring photographs from the collection. The work has also appeared in numerous group shows including "A Century of Black Photography," and recent one-person shows have been held at institutions including the Denver Art Museum; the Detroit Historical Museum; the Parsons School of Design; the Museum of Art, Rhode Island School of Design; and the Rochester Institute of Technology. The funds earned by the collection are used for its maintenance.

The management of the collection—choosing negatives for reference and exhibition-quality prints, monitoring print quality, and selecting exhibition sites and the rights to reproduce work — has always involved a close three-way collaborative effort. The preparation of this book followed the same pattern. We come from diverse backgrounds and bring different kinds of expertise to this project: Milt is the musician, jazz historian and documentarian; David, a lifelong friend of Milt's, is a sociologist who specializes in music; and Holly is a conservator of works of art and documents on paper.

When we began work on this project, we optimistically thought we could select two hundred high-quality photographs for the book. In the early stages we identified more than fourteen hundred photographs for possible inclusion, and after extensive editing we reduced the number to about six hundred. At that point, we realized that although we could make additional cuts, there was no rational way to select two hundred photographs. After discussing our alternatives, we proposed to our publisher that we plan for a second book. Fortunately, Katie and Tom Burke at Pomegranate were extremely receptive to our idea. We agreed that the first book (*OverTime*) would contain more than fifty personality galleries, while the second would be organized by instrument—trumpet players, drummers, bassists, and so on.

Needless to say, in the course of choosing photographs for the present book, we had to make selections for the second publication. In the process, we balanced personal, historical, technical and aesthetic factors. We wanted to make sure that the vast number of musicians Milt has known and worked with were represented, we wanted to include significant figures in the jazz world, and we wanted to use photographs that were both technically sound and aesthetically pleasing.

Obviously, it was impossible to include all the musicians Milt has known. In some cases, no photographs were available. In other instances, considera- tion was given to whether photographs had been previously published. Where we knew that there were few photographs ever taken of a major jazz figure, or where Milt recorded an unusual combination of personalities, we went to extraordinary lengths to obtain a print. When this occurred, technical and aesthetic aspects of the photograph became secondary.

We also decided to include photographs of Milt himself. He would frequently hand his camera to a bystander to take his picture. Although photographic credit cannot be attributed for these shots, all but two of the pictures of Milt are taken from film that was in his camera.

It is important to recognize that Milt has never been a professional photographer. Although he has taken thousands of pictures, he readily acknowledges that many are of uncertain quality. This can be explained by the way he took, processed, and eventually stored his pho- tographs. He rarely used a flash in low-light situations, and to be less obtrusive he often preset the camera's focus so he could literally shoot from the hip. Many rolls of film remained undeveloped for twenty years. And because Milt was rarely in the darkroom, at times he inadvertently used stale chemicals to process his film. Negatives were paper-clipped to contact prints, which resulted in rust problems, and a flooded basement caused many to adhere to one another and to their paper sleeves. In recent years some of the older negatives have begun to deteriorate. The only satisfactory solution has been to produce copy negatives.

Despite all of these limitations, the unique character of Milt's photographs is immediately recognizable. He brings an honest intimacy and an insider's point of view to an unusual, truly American subculture.

Personality Galleries

Louis Armstrong

Louis was born in New Orleans, but he moved to Chicago and became a star when I was still in knee pants. I was overjoyed when he asked me to join his band in the early '50s. Playing with him and getting to know him was a dream come true. Music was his life, and he communicated his love to audiences around the world better than anyone I've ever known.

Unknown, Lucille Armstrong and Louis Armstrong, Honolulu, Hawaii, c. 1954

Gene Krupa, Trummy Young, Peanuts Hucko, Louis Armstrong, Bobby Hackett and Mort Herbert, television studio, New York, 1959

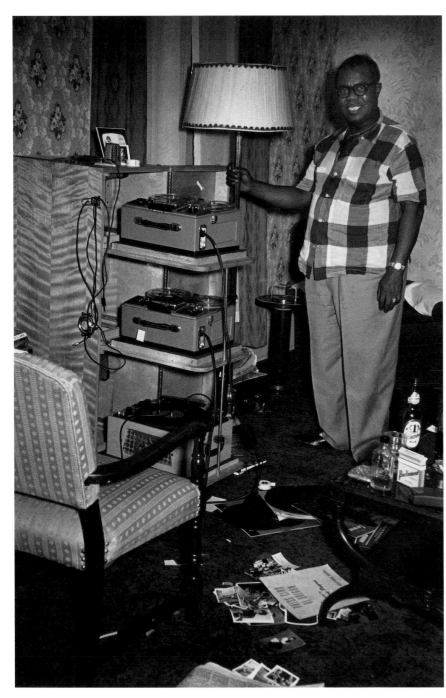

Louis Armstrong, hotel room, Seattle, 1954

Louis Armstrong and Milt Hinton, Japan, c. 1953

Billy Kyle, unknown, Bobby Hackett, Louis Armstrong, Jackie Gleason and Trummy Young, television studio, New York, 1959

Danny Barker

I've known Danny since the late '30s when he joined Cab. He and his wife are from New Orleans, and in the early '50s when they lived in New York, they fed dozens of musicians who came up from their hometown and were struggling to make it. He moved back to New Orleans about thirty years ago, and he's been working with young people there, passing on the jazz tradition he knows so well to future generations.

Danny Barker, Springfield, Illinois, c. 1945

Danny Barker and Preston Jackson, New Orleans, c. 1979

Foreground: Danny Barker and Jerome Darr; at the bar: Barney Bigard (checkered overcoat); background: Willie "The Lion" Smith, Beefsteak Charlie's, New York, c. 1955

Count Basie

Basie and I lived around the corner from each other for many years, and our wives were dear friends. In the early '50s he asked me to join the band. By that time I was already busy in the studios, but I told him I'd do it whenever he was playing in the New York area, just as long as he picked me up and drove me home every night. He must've been desperate, because he agreed. It was probably the most unusual arrangement a well-known bandleader ever made with a bass player.

Ben Webster, Count Basie, Roy Eldridge, Dickie Wells and Doc Cheatham, television studio, New York, 1957

Count Basie, rehearsal, New York, c. 1958

Teddy Rigg, Red Allen, Pee Wee Russell, Count Basie, Freddie Green, Lester Young, Ed Jones, Rex Stewart and Jo Jones, television studio, New York, 1957

Count Basie, television studio, New York, 1957

Count Basie, Jo Jones, Freddie Green (partially hidden), Ed Jones (back to camera), Doc Cheatham, Joe Newman, Gerry Mulligan (back to camera), Dickie Wells, Roy Eldridge and Emmett Berry, television studio, New York, 1957

Louie Bellson

I worked with Pearl Bailey in the '70s and '80s, so I got a chance to play with Louie quite often. His father owned a music store in Illinois, and the way he tells it, from birth he was consumed with drums. He's a very disciplined person. He practices constantly and works hard on his solos. There's no question he's gotten results. He's one of our strongest big band drummers and one of the nicest human beings in the world.

Louie Bellson and students, Camp Concord, Concord, California, c. 1972

Louie Bellson, aboard the Norway, *1988*

Chu Berry

Chu replaced Ben Webster in Cab's band. He was a different kind of player, but every bit as good, and he had a strong influence on the music we played. He made sure we got new tunes and arrangements, and he got Cab to hire young talents like Dizzy. Chu was only thirty-one when he died in a car accident, but he'd already developed a big following. Had he lived longer, I know he'd be a legend on a par with giants like Coleman Hawkins, Ben Webster and Lester Young.

Chu Berry, unknown, Danny Barker and Lamar Wright, Durham, North Carolina, c. 1940

Dizzy Gillespie, Chu Berry and Quentin Jackson, Fox Theater, Detroit, c. 1940

Chu Berry and unknown woman and child, Alabama, c. 1939

Barney Bigard

Barney was a magnificent gentleman I got to spend time with when we were both working for Louis. He and Louis had strong ties from their days in New Orleans, and from what I saw, Louis always seemed to want Barney's approval. If someone asked Louis to do something he wasn't sure about, he always looked to Barney for direction. I think it had something to do with social class, which came from the old days in New Orleans.

Unknown, Barney Bigard, Bernie Privin and Jimmy Maxwell, New Orleans, c. 1978

Jack and Herman (bartenders), Barney Bigard and unknown, Beefsteak Charlie's, New York, c. 1955

Eubie Blake

I was twenty-three when I performed with Eubie the first time. He was conducting a concert at the Chicago World's Fair celebrating the anniversary of the signing of the Emancipation Proclamation. Sixty years later I played the concert that honored him on his one hundredth birthday. Eubie helped bring a new kind of dignity to jazz by introducing it into Broadway theaters and exposing people around the world to it.

Eubie Blake and Noble Sissle, recording studio, New York, c. 1958

Panama Francis, Eubie Blake, Kenny Burrell and Buster Bailey, recording studio, New York, c. 1958

Eubie Blake and Milt Hinton, Nice, France, c. 1978

Eubie Blake, Colorado Springs, Colorado, c. 1978

Eubie Blake, The White House, Washington, D.C., 1978

Ray Brown

Ray's the bass guru. He does it all. He's one of those musicians who has a sound and a style that's immediately recognizable. He's also a great quarterback—one of the few bass players I know who can lead any kind of group, no matter whether it's a trio or a big band. And to top it off, he's a great teacher, too.

Billy Eckstine, Ray Brown and Hank Jones, Moscow, Idaho, 1991

Billy Eckstine, Ray Brown and Hank Jones, Moscow, Idaho, 1991

Jo Jones, Duke Ellington and Ray Brown, Yale University, New Haven, Connecticut, 1972

Kenny Burrell

During the '50s and '60s, Kenny and I worked together in the New York studios. Sometimes we'd play a rock 'n' roll session in the morning, do a date with a popular singer in the afternoon, and end the day making a record with a jazz vocalist like Joe Williams. You had to be versatile and proficient at reading music to do this kind of work. Kenny had no problem. What made him extra special was that he continued developing as an innovative jazz player.

Kenny Burrell, recording studio, New York, c. 1960

Kenny Burrell, recording studio, New York, c. 1962

Hank Jones and Kenny Burrell, Sarasota, Florida, c. 1984

Cab Calloway

Cab is my musical father. When he hired me I got a chance to make it in the big leagues—traveling around the country and playing with some of the greatest musicians of the day. He only had a few simple rules for the band. Most important was being on time. Just before a rehearsal would end he'd say, "Remember, I gotta be there tonight, so you'd *better* be there." He led by example, and if you followed him, there was never any problem.

Hilton Jefferson and Cab Calloway, Boston, c. 1941

Lamar Wright, Mario Bauza, Foots Thomas, Eddie Morton, Cab Calloway and Benny Payne, train station, Atlanta, c. 1940

Cab Calloway and Charlotte Hinton, Miami, Florida, c.1951

Cab Calloway, Milt Hinton and Mona Hinton, Nice, France, c. 1981

Dizzy Gillespie, Panama Francis and Cab Calloway, recording studio, New Jersey, 1990

Benny Carter

Not many people talk about it today, but Benny had a wonderful band back in the '30s. All the guys wanted to join because he was so experimental—just like Duke and Fletcher. He knows every aspect of music, so his band was a place where musicians could learn. In the old days, it was common knowledge—no matter how good you were, after a stint in Benny's band, you'd be even better.

John Frigo and Benny Carter, Denver, Colorado, c. 1985

Marshall Royal, Benny Carter and Bob Wilber, Colorado Springs, Colorado, c. 1978

Ron Carter

Ron's training has made him comfortable playing either classical music or jazz. His dexterity amazes me. He handles a bass like it's a violin, and he's one of the few bass players I recognize after hearing only a couple of bars. Musicians like Ron give me hope for the future. He's learned the jazz tradition, and he's building on it. He's also aware of the responsibility of passing on his knowledge to future generations.

Mrs. Ismay Duvivier and Ron Carter, Fat Tuesday's, New York, 1991

Stanley Turrentine and Ron Carter, The White House, Washington, D.C., c. 1981

Ron Carter and Bob Cranshaw, New York, c. 1971

Doc Cheatham

Doc was in Cab's band when I joined in 1936, and he already had a reputation. He'd toured Europe with Sam Wooding and done endorsements for Selma trumpets. He played so beautifully. I can still hear his solo on "Cotton," where he was featured with Claude Jones on trombone. Knowing Doc for more than half a century has been a true learning experience.

Milt Hinton and Doc Cheatham, Santa Fe, New Mexico, 1990

Doc Cheatham, Mona Hinton and unknown, Sir John Motel, Miami, Florida, c. 1950

Eddie Gomez, Wynton Marsalis and Doc Cheatham, rehearsal, Town Hall, New York, 1990

Sweets Edison

I think the first time I got to hang out with Sweets was when he came to New York with Basie in 1936 or '37. He was a sharp dresser, and even back then he had the makings of an unique musical style. Through the years he's developed a sound that's immediately recognizable on all kinds of records in both jazz and popular music.

Sweets Edison and Clark Terry, concert, Bern, Switzerland, 1988

Sweets Edison and Snooky Young, Denver, Colorado, c. 1986

Sweets Edison and Terence Blanchard, recording studio, New York, 1991

Roy Eldridge

I first got to play with Roy when I was working at the Three Deuces in Chicago with Zutty Singleton. It was 1936. Roy was with Fletcher, and whenever the band was in town he'd come by and jam after hours. By that time I'd worked with Freddie Keppard and Jabbo Smith, and I knew Louis's playing, of course. Roy had a different sound. He was more modern, but he still played hot and he was exciting to watch.

Roy Eldridge and Jimmy Nottingham, recording studio, New York, c. 1961

Roy Eldridge, backstage, Florida, c. 1986

Ben Webster, Count Basie, Roy Eldridge, Dickie Wells, Doc Cheatham and Gerry Mulligan, television studio, New York, 1957

George Wettling, Pee Wee Russell, Roy Eldridge, Marty Napoleon and Big Chief Moore, Metropole Cafe, New York, c. 1955

Eric Dixon, Roy Eldridge and Al Grey, rehearsal, New York, c. 1968

Osie Johnson, Jimmy Rushing and Roy Eldridge, television studio, New York, 1957

Duke Ellington

For most of my life, Duke's band was *the* band. If he'd asked me to join him when I was with Cab, I would've gone in a minute. The glamour and the musical challenge were beyond comparison. There was a rumor that he and Cab had an unwritten agreement about not hiring each other's musicians. There may be some truth to it because after I'd left Cab and was freelancing in the studios, Duke would call me to do record dates with him. Unfortunately, I always had some other commitment and had to turn him down.

Unknown, Earle Warren, Duke Ellington and Jo Jones, French Embassy, New York, c. 1973

Willie "The Lion" Smith and Duke Ellington, The White House, Washington, D.C., 1969

Pee Wee Erwin

Pee Wee was one of the great trumpet players of my era. He worked with some of the best bands of the '30s—Isham Jones, Freddy Martin, Benny Goodman, Ray Noble and Tommy Dorsey. Through the years we played dozens of jazz festivals and parties together. It was always a treat to be on the stand with him because we liked the same kind of happy music. We all miss him tremendously.

Pee Wee Erwin and Vic Dickenson, recording studio, New York, c. 1971

Bob Wilber and Pee Wee Erwin, Odessa, Texas, c. 1976

Pee Wee Erwin and Pug Wilber, Scottsdale, Arizona, c. 1980

Jon Faddis

Jon is one of the great trumpet players of the jazz world. He has a lot of the traits I'm seeing in the new breed of jazz musicians—he knows his history, he knows his instrument, he's got warmth, he lives a healthy life and he's always willing to help other musicians.

Jon Faddis, Gracie Mansion, New York, c. 1983

Jon Faddis, Gracie Mansion, New York, c. 1983

Jon Faddis, Gracie Mansion, New York, c. 1983

Chuck Mangione, Jon Faddis and Joe Newman, Gracie Mansion, New York, c. 1983

Art Farmer

I've known Art since the early '50s when we rehearsed George Russell's Lydian compositions together. And a few years later we recorded John Benson Brooks's *Alabama Concerto* with Cannonball and Barry Galbraith. Of course, Art's been a great creative force in jazz, but most people don't know he's also a fantastic reader—one of the best I've ever known. That's a special talent very few people have.

Waymon Reed and Art Farmer, Bern, Switzerland, c. 1983

Art Farmer, recording studio, New York, c. 1962

Jimmy Cleveland, Gerry Mulligan, Bill Crow and Art Farmer, television studio, New York, c. 1956

Dizzy Gillespie

Diz was a kid when he joined Cab's band in the late '30s. Many guys in the band laughed at his playing, but a few of us who listened recognized that he was way ahead of his time. He was always willing to share his knowledge. Sometimes when we worked the Cotton Club and the weather was warm, the two of us would take our instruments up to the roof during intermissions. He'd show me some of his chord inventions and get me to try new ways of playing.

Dizzy Gillespie, Palace Theater, Cleveland, Ohio, 1939

Danny Barker and Dizzy Gillespie, c. 1940

Willie "The Lion" Smith, Dizzy Gillespie and Eubie Blake, Newport, Rhode Island, c.1971

Dizzy Gillespie, Pori, Finland, 1990

Dizzy Gillespie, Pori, Finland, 1990

Dizzy Gillespie, television studio, New York, 1959

Clark Terry, Dizzy Gillespie and Urbie Green, The White House, Washington, D.C., 1969

Dizzy Gillespie and Major Holley, The Hague, The Netherlands, 1990

Tyree Glenn

For a couple of years a few of us in Cab's band—Tyree, Hilton Jefferson, Paul Webster and I—got involved in playing bridge. We'd study the bridge column in the papers every day and we'd have regular games on the train or backstage in some theater. What I remember most about those games is the way we'd talk to each other. Instead of using our vulgar pinochle language, we'd try to be more refined. I can still hear Tyree saying, "Sugarloafs, why did you trump my ace?"

Tyree Glenn and son Roger, New York, c. 1947

Tyree Glenn, unknown and Foots Thomas, Montevideo, Uruguay, 1950

Tyree Glenn, recording studio, New York, c. 1972

Benny Goodman

Benny and I first met in Chicago in 1923. We were both thirteen and studying music at Jane Addams's Hull House for twenty-five cents a lesson. We performed and recorded together, on and off, for five decades, and although we argued from time to time, I know we always respected each other musically.

Bucky Pizzarelli and Benny Goodman, recording studio, New York c. 1976

Benny Goodman, concert at Macy's, New York, c. 1955

Benny Goodman, recording studio, New York, c.1976

Scott Hamilton

Scott couldn't have been more than twenty the first time I saw him in New York. I was playing at Michael's Pub with Hank Jones when he came by one night and asked to sit in. With his slicked-back hair and double-breasted suit, he looked like a holdover from the '40s. But we gave him a blood test, and he passed with flying colors. He knew all the tunes—old and new—and a few weeks later he had his own group booked at the same place.

Scott and Manami Hamilton, Denver, Colorado, c. 1983

Scott Hamilton, Colorado Springs, Colorado, c. 1979

Scott Hamilton, Flip Phillips and Howard Alden, Denver, Colorado, c. 1987

Lionel Hampton

Gates and I grew up together in Chicago, and we were both in a band sponsored by the *Chicago Defender* that was directed by Major N. Clark Smith. In fact, Gates tried to keep me out of the band because I was still in short pants and he was wearing trousers. And a few years later I did the same thing to Nat Cole. We still talk about the discipline and musical training we got from Major Smith. The foundation he provided his students has served us well.

Unknown and Lionel Hampton, Washington, D.C., c. 1985

Jane Jarvis and Lionel Hampton, Zinno's, New York, c. 1988

Louie Bellson and Lionel Hampton, rehearsal, Rochester, New York, 1981

Coleman Hawkins

When Bean came back from Europe everyone was anxious to hear how he sounded. Someone arranged to have a breakfast session at Puss Johnson's in Harlem. It started about 5:00 A.M. Prez and Ben Webster were there along with the regular house band. Prez went on first with his own rhythm section of Jo Jones and Walter Page. Ben went on next with me and Cozy accompanying him. Bean was last, and I truthfully don't recall who played for him. He took no prisoners. By eleven in the morning there was no question—he was still king of the tenors.

Coleman Hawkins, television studio, New York, 1957

Maxine Sullivan, Joe Thomas, Stuff Smith and Coleman Hawkins, Harlem, New York, 1959

Eddie Bert and Coleman Hawkins, recording studio, New York, c. 1955

Billie Holiday

I did a few record dates with Billie in the late '30s, and I also made her last sessions in 1959. Through the years I've performed and recorded with hundreds of singers, and no one ever came close. In the early days she had it all—the voice, the phrasing and the emotion. Later, even though her voice had lost its softness, she could still deliver a song like no one else.

Billie Holiday, recording studio, New York, 1959

Billie Holiday and Hank Jones, recording studio, New York, 1959

Billie Holiday, recording studio, New York, 1959

Unknown, Freddie Green, Count Basie, Billie Holiday and Jo Jones, television studio, New York, 1957

Major Holley

Mule was very influential in the development of jazz bass playing. What always amazed me about him was his ability to take the worst bass in the world—something a step away from a cigar box—and make it sound beautiful. He had one of the deepest and most powerful voices I've ever heard. He could be gruff at times, but underneath that exterior was a heart of gold.

Major Holley, Nice, France, c. 1979

Major Holley and Ron Carter, rehearsal, New York, 1990

Major Holley, Don Butterfield and Rudy Powell, recording studio, New York, c. 1960

Dick Hyman

Dick's very knowledgeable about all aspects of music. He's at home with either classical music or jazz, and he's a gifted writer, arranger and educator. He also has a thorough comprehension of the evolution of the piano in jazz, and with his amazing technique and dexterity as a pianist, he's comfortable playing all the styles.

Dick Hyman and Roy Hamilton, recording studio, New York, c. 1956

Patti LaBelle and Dick Hyman, rehearsal, Washington, D.C., c. 1983

Kenny Davern and Dick Hyman, rehearsal, Sarasota, Florida, c. 1986

Milt Jackson

I've known Milt Jackson forever. I'll never forget the time I ran into him in Cuba. It was back in the early '50s, and I was with Cab at one of the big hotels in Havana. One afternoon I was walking down a wide avenue and I stumbled into four or five guys from Woody Herman's band including Shelly Manne and Milt. After we got over the shock of seeing each other a thousand miles from home, we carried on for an hour, acting like we were on the corner of 48th and Broadway.

Milt Jackson and Dizzy Gillespie, Nice, France, c. 1979

Milt Jackson, Dizzy Gillespie and unknown, Nice, France, c. 1979

Milt Jackson and Dizzy Gillespie, Nice, France, c. 1979

Charlie Persip, Milt Jackson, Horace Silver and Percy Heath, Newport, Rhode Island, c. 1956

Hilton Jefferson

I first got to know Jeff when he joined Cab's band in 1940, and over the years he became one of my dearest friends. He was a musicians' musician, known and respected by other players but practically unknown by the public. He was too shy to push his own career, but there's no question he had the ability. Benny Carter once called him his favorite alto player. Listen to Jeff's solo on "Willow Weep for Me" and it's not hard to understand why.

Phil Woods and Hilton Jefferson, recording studio, New York, c. 1957

George Dorsey, Hilton Jefferson, unknown and Prince Robinson, recording studio, New York, c. 1958

Budd Johnson

Budd was my best friend Keg's younger brother. He was a great tenor player and a good arranger who did a lot of work for Earl Hines's band. At one point, Keg brought him into Cab's band, but that didn't last long. Eventually, he got known around 52nd Street, playing bebop with some of the greats. He was always very popular, and he had a solid following.

Eddie "Lockjaw" Davis, Eddie Bert and Budd Johnson, Colorado Springs, Colorado, c. 1977

Budd Johnson, Eddie Durham and Edgar Battle, backstage, Carnegie Hall, New York, c. 1972

Budd Johnson, recording studio, New York, c. 1972

Osie Johnson

Osie was an all-around musician who was way ahead of his time. In addition to drums, he could play saxophone and piano. He also sang and wrote wonderful arrangements. When I was in the studios I did a lot of work with Barry Galbraith, Hank Jones and Osie. We had a reputation for being able to play any kind of music and improvise arrangements on the spot. I've never known people like those guys. Not only was their musicianship impeccable, but they could work under pressure and be amiable and relaxed at the same time.

Barry Galbraith and Osie Johnson, recording studio, New York, c. 1958

Osie Johnson and Wendell Marshall, recording studio, New York, c. 1960

Osie Johnson, recording studio, New York, c. 1964

Jo Jones

The way Jo played drums showed me that there's more to being in a rhythm section than just keeping time. He was a trap drummer, a natural like Buddy Rich, and he was amazingly versatile. He listened to soloists and learned their particular musical style. That way, whenever they were featured, he'd adjust his playing to make them sound better. The greatest compliment about him I ever heard came from another great drummer, Max Roach. He said, "For every three beats a drummer plays, two belong to Jo Jones."

Jo Jones, recording studio, New York, c. 1972

Jo Jones, recording studio, New York, c. 1956

Big Maybelle, Edmond Hall and Jo Jones, rehearsal, New York, c. 1971

Danny Barker and Jo Jones, television studio, New York, 1957

Duke Ellington and Jo Jones, Yale University, New Haven, Connecticut, 1972

Quincy Jones

I was on one of Q's first record dates when the copyist was late with the music and the date had to go overtime. Q was the arranger, so he was responsible for paying all the overtime salaries. Since he was just starting out, when I got my check I tore it in half and sent it back to him. I didn't know it until recently, but he'd had that check framed and it's been hanging on his office wall for more than thirty-five years.

Quincy Jones, recording studio, New York, c. 1957

Quincy Jones and Osie Johnson, recording studio, New York, c. 1965

Quincy Jones, Phil Moore and unknown, recording studio, New York, 1959

Phil Woods, Sol Gubin and Quincy Jones, recording studio, New York, c. 1960

Jerome Richardson, Quincy Jones, unknown and Sam Jones, Stamford, Connecticut, c. 1965

Gene Krupa

I met Gene in the late '30s when he was working with Benny Goodman at the Pennsylvania Hotel and I was with Cab at the Cotton Club. He was a great drummer who was highly successful, but he probably had the worst luck of anybody in music—family troubles, a devastating fire and some highly publicized legal problems. Despite it all he remained a gentleman, always courteous and never insisting on being treated like a star.

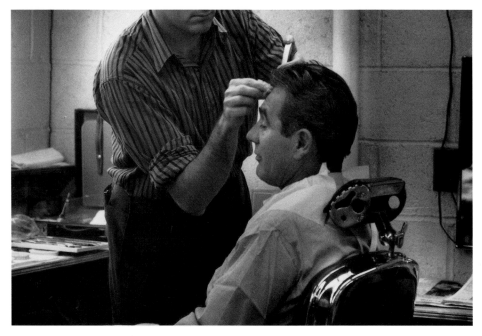

Gene Krupa, television studio, New York, c. 1964

Bobby Hackett, Jackie Gleason, Louis Armstrong and Gene Krupa, television studio, New York, 1959

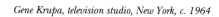

Gene Krupa, television studio, New York, c. 1964

Gene Krupa, recording studio, New York, c. 1967

(4th row) Buck Clayton, Hilton Jefferson, Benny Golson, Wilbur Ware, Chubby Jackson and Johnny Griffin; (3rd row) Miff Mole, Zutty Singleton, Red Allen, Taft Jordan, Art Blakey and Charlie Mingus; (2nd row) Jo Jones and Gene Krupa; (1st row) Roy Eldridge, George Wettling and Horace Silver, Harlem, New York, 1959

Bill Lee

Bill's an incredible talent. In addition to bass, he plays piano and he writes beautifully. In the late '60s he had the vision to form the New York Bass Violin Choir, an unusual group with six bass players. He was dealing with some of the busiest musicians in New York, but he was determined to bring us together. He wrote for the group like we were a string quartet. We all loved the experience and were grateful to him for making it possible.

Joie Lee and Bill Lee, New York, c. 1971

Bill Lee and Spike Lee, recording studio, New York, c. 1987

Bill Lee, Richard Davis, Ron Carter, Michael Fleming and Lisle Atkinson, rehearsal, New York, c. 1970

Branford Marsalis

Branford's a great experimenter. He tries everything musically. Since he plays tenor, he's particularly interested in the pioneers of his instrument. Delfeo's actually the one who first heard some of my records of Chu Berry and made tapes of them for his older brother. A few months later, Branford asked me to record with him, and *Trio Jeepy* is the result.

Wynton Marsalis and Branford Marsalis, New Orleans, c. 1979

Milt Hinton, Branford Marsalis and Jeff Watts, New York, c. 1989

Wynton Marsalis

The first time I met Wynton he was in his early teens. I was in New Orleans doing a clinic at his father's school, and he was one of the students. Since then, I've performed with him many times. He's a well-disciplined musician and a perfectionist. He's no frills—he's honest and direct—and he has great respect for the jazz tradition and for his elders in the jazz world.

Wynton Marsalis, Dick Hyman and Marty Napoleon, rehearsal, New York, c. 1988

Wynton Marsalis, Frank Wess and Todd Williams, rehearsal, New York, c. 1989

Jay McShann

Jay McShann is a true Kansas City blues piano player with a voice to match. He's been playing for more than sixty years, so he's lived through most of jazz history. He's seen it all, and he's played with the legends before and after Charlie Parker.

Sir Roland Hanna and Jay McShann, Denver, Colorado, c. 1986

Jay McShann, Chicago, c. 1983

Jay McShann and Roger Kellaway, Scottsdale, Arizona, c. 1981

Jay McShann and Ralph Sutton, concert, Minneapolis, Minnesota, c. 1989

Charlie Mingus

The first time I met Charlie I was with Cab, and he challenged me to play complicated bass parts from a well-known exercise book. After he found out I could read better, we became close friends. Years later, whenever he needed more than one bass for a record or a concert, he'd call me. His music was avant garde and very eccentric, but he was brilliant. One of the greatest compliments I ever got was what he wrote in the copy of his autobiography he gave me. It says, "To my teacher."

Willie Ruff, Joe Benjamin and Charlie Mingus, Yale University, New Haven, Connecticut, 1972

Charlie Mingus and Milt Hinton, Philadelphia, c. 1972

Danny Richmond and Charlie Mingus, rehearsal, New York, c. 1963

Charles McPhearson, Lee Konitz, Dick Griffin, Eddie Bert, unknown and Charlie Mingus, Philadelphia, c. 1972

Unknown, Charlie Mingus, unknown, unknown, Philadelphia, c. 1972

Eddie Bert, unknown, Charlie Mingus and George Wein, rehearsal, New York, c. 1963

Gerry Mulligan

Whenever there was good jazz being played—in a club, at a concert, on television—Gerry Mulligan was there. He's been a mainstay in the jazz world for forty years.

Gerry Mulligan, television studio, New York, 1957

Gerry Mulligan, Freddie Green and Jo Jones, television studio, New York, 1957

Gerry Mulligan, United Nations, New York, c. 1981

Ike Quebec

I worked with Quee in Cab's band in the '40s. About twenty years later, I made a couple of wonderful albums with him. He was one of my favorite musicians. He had a big sound, like Coleman Hawkins, but his playing was even more soulful.

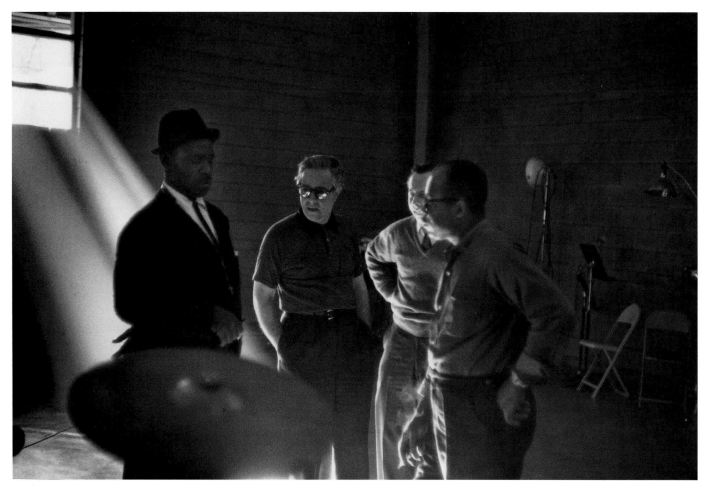

Ike Quebec, Alfred Lyons, Frank Wolff and Al Harewood, recording studio, New York, c. 1962

Freddy Roach and Ike Quebec, recording studio, New York, c. 1962

Red Rodney

Red's got a fascinating story. He's one of very few whites who was really involved in the bebop scene. There's no question he survived a disastrous period of jazz history. He was down at the bottom but managed to climb back up. Red still has great chops, and he's in constant demand. He's proud of everything he's accomplished, and he should be.

Red Rodney and Derek Smith, recording studio, New York, 1991

Red Rodney, recording studio, New York, 1991

Jimmy Rushing

I never knew Jimmy very well, but in the late '50s and '60s whenever he'd record I'd usually get the call. I remember playing on his last date. Dave Frishberg was there along with Ray Nance. In fact, I recorded a duet with Ray playing violin. We were thrilled because we'd played violin at the same high school and the experience reminded us of the old days.

Jimmy Rushing, television studio, New York, 1957

Jimmy Rushing, recording studio, New York, c. 1955

Coleman Hawkins, Jimmy Rushing, Gerry Mulligan (partially hidden), Count Basie, Freddie Green, Ed Jones, Vic Dickenson, Benny Morton (partially hidden), Dickie Wells and Jo Jones, television studio, New York, 1957

Pee Wee Russell

Pee Wee was the first clarinet player I heard who worked in Dixieland bands but didn't play Dixieland. He used different, more modern changes, almost like Monk, and he did it very well. He was a real character, and one of the few white guys who hung out in Beefsteak Charlie's on a regular basis.

Pee Wee Russell, outside the Metropole Cafe, New York, c. 1952

Pee Wee Russell, Metropole Cafe, New York, c. 1955

Irv Manning, George Wettling, Willie "The Lion" Smith, Pee Wee Russell, Red Allen and J.C. Higgenbotham, television studio, New York, 1959

Sylvia Sims

Sylvia's a true artist. Whenever she performs there are always other singers in the audience, listening and learning. To me, there's no greater compliment.

Sylvia Sims and Howard Alden, recording studio, New York, 1990

Sylvia Sims, recording studio, New York, 1990

Zoot Sims

Zoot was the salt of the earth. Playing came naturally to him. He wasn't academic, and he didn't know chords. He just did it with a style all his own. That's true genius.

Zoot Sims and Phil Woods, recording studio, New York, c. 1959

Zoot Sims, New Orleans, c. 1979

Joe Temperley and Zoot Sims, recording studio, New York, c. 1977

Buddy Tate

Buddy's always been a sleek, dapper man. He has a big, wonderful sound, and he's a fantastic showman.

Buddy Tate, recording studio, New York, c. 1975

Buddy Tate, recording studio, New York, c.1982

Clark Terry

Cee Tee has a sound and style that's immediately identifiable. Throughout his career—with Duke, in the studios, with his own bands—he's worked hard at perfecting his musical knowledge. He's a true jazz artist and also one of the best teachers I've ever seen. He knows how to work with young people, and he's very unselfish about sharing what he knows. It's a learning experience for me whenever I'm around him.

Clark Terry and Willie Cook, concert, New York, c. 1956

Bernie Glow and Clark Terry, recording studio, New York, c. 1955

Clark Terry, Sarasota, Florida, c. 1987

Clark Terry, Odessa, Texas, c. 1975

Ashley Alexander and Clark Terry, Odessa, Texas, c. 1975

Clark Terry, Dizzy Gillespie and Oscar Peterson, concert, Bern, Switzerland, 1988

Warren Vaché

Warren's one of the best young players around today. When he was first starting out, Pee Wee Erwin took him under his wing. In recent years, he's really blossomed. He's gained a lot of power, plays prettier and has developed a style that's all his own.

Warren Vaché, Bern, Switzerland, 1989

Dick Hyman, Karen Brown and Warren Vaché, recording studio, New York, c. 1989

Warren Vaché, Gus Johnson and Ralph Sutton, Bern, Switzerland, 1989

Joe Venuti

Joe had a reputation for practical jokes, but he had a serious side, too. He had no patience for prejudice, especially when it involved musicians. I know he got Eddie South jobs at fancy places where black musicians couldn't work. He'd tell owners the only way they'd get him back was to hire Eddie. Joe did some pretty courageous things long before it was popular.

Joe Venuti, recording studio, New York, c. 1975

Joe Venuti, Yank Lawson, Bucky Pizzarelli, Billy Butterfield, unknown and Willis Conover, Colorado Springs, Colorado, c. 1975

Joe Venuti and Bucky Pizzarelli, rehearsal, Carnegie Hall, New York, c. 1977

Joe Venuti, Michael's Pub, New York, c. 1973

Joe Venuti, Michael's Pub, New York, c. 1973

Joe Venuti and Bobby Rosengarden, Honolulu, Hawaii, c. 1977

Dinah Washington

Dinah was a true musician. Back in the '50s and '60s a record session lasted three hours and you were allowed to record up to three tunes during that time period. Some singers couldn't even finish one song in three hours, but Dinah was different. The band would spend most of a session rehearsing without her. Finally, with twenty minutes left, she'd walk in, do one take each on three tunes, and we'd be finished.

Barry Galbraith, Don Elliott, Dinah Washington and Ernie Wilkins, recording studio, New York, c.1956

Dinah Washington, recording studio, New York, c. 1958

Cecil Payne and Dinah Washington, recording studio, New York, c. 1963

Ben Webster

I met Ben the day I joined Cab's band in 1936. He was a star back then, but he still took a special interest in me. He'd take me along to play for him at after-hours clubs, and he'd show me how to develop better bass lines. The day I arrived in New York with the band for the first time, he even took me to a clothing store, just to make sure I looked sharp enough to hang out with him in the big city.

Paul Webster, Ben Webster and Milt Hinton, Harlem, New York, c. 1941

Paul Webster, Ben Webster and Milt Hinton, Harlem, New York, c. 1941

Ben Webster, Harlem, New York, c. 1941

Ben Webster, Earle Warren, Count Basie, Ed Jones, Coleman Hawkins and Freddie Green, television studio, New York, 1957

Ben Webster, Beefsteak Charlie's, New York, c. 1960

Paul Webster and Ben Webster, Beefsteak Charlie's, New York, c. 1960

Joe Williams

Joe and I spent a lot of time making music together when we were growing up in Chicago. We still laugh about the three dollars a night we'd get for playing local dances. He's easy to work with because he knows what he wants musically and he can explain it to his musicians. He's never been like so many others who changed styles and gave in to fads when they became popular, and over the years his voice has mellowed beautifully.

George Avakian, Joe Williams and Oliver Nelson, recording studio, New York, c. 1966

Joe Williams, recording studio, New York, c. 1966

Hank Jones, Joe Williams and Kenny Burrell, recording studio, New York, c. 1966

Joe Williams and B.B. King, Bern, Switzerland, 1988

Joe Williams and Frank Foster, Bern, Switzerland, 1988

Billy Eckstine, Lou Rawls, Joe Williams, Gerry Mulligan and Clark Terry, The White House, Washington, D.C., 1970

Teddy Wilson

I first got friendly with Teddy in Chicago in 1933. He'd come up from Texas with a few other good musicians like Keg and Budd Johnson. Later that year he left for New York to join Benny Carter, but Teddy never forgot our friendship. I'll always be grateful to him for hiring me to play on some of those great record dates in the late '30s.

Teddy Wilson and son Theodore, studio, New York, c. 1955

Teddy Wilson, studio, New York, c. 1955

Theodore Wilson, Jr., Teddy Wilson and Stephen Wilson, Boston, c. 1979

Teddy Wilson, rehearsal, Rochester, New York, 1981

Teddy Wilson, studio, New York, c. 1955

Teddy Wilson, recording studio, New York, c. 1975

Phil Woods

I worked with Phil in the studios back in the '50s and '60s. He was consumed by jazz. He would have preferred to play his own music day and night, but he had to do record dates to get by financially. He's one of the greatest alto players I ever heard, but I never thought he got nearly the recognition he deserved.

Phil Woods, recording studio, New York, c. 1958

Phil Woods, Colorado Springs, Colorado, c. 1981

Phil Bodner and Phil Woods, recording studio, New York, c. 1963

Lester Young

Prez is a legend throughout the world. When I was in Moscow in the early '80s a young Russian walked up to me on the street and said, "I am a member of the Lester Young Jazz Club in Moscow." Then he handed me a button with a picture of Prez wearing his porkpie. I'd never heard of a Lester Young Club in the States, but there I was, more than halfway around the world, hearing about a group dedicated to Prez and his music.

Lester Young and Freddie Green, television studio, New York, 1957

Lester Young and J.C. Heard, Harlem, New York, 1959

Lester Young, Earle Warren, Coleman Hawkins and Gerry Mulligan, television studio, New York, 1957

Photographic
Index